MW01152372

Sing 'n Learn™
JAPANESE 1
うたで ならおう にほんご

Introduce Japanese with Favorite Children's Songs

By Tazuko Inui and Selina Yoon
Illustrations by Nguyen Thi Hop

MASTER
COMMUNICATIONS

Published by Master Communications, P.O. Box 9096, Cincinnati, Ohio 45209-0096 U.S.A.

Printed in the United States of America.
ISBN 1-888194-21-9 (Book and Cassette)
ISBN 1-888194-22-7 (Book and CD)
Library of Congress Catalog Card Number: 98-68414

Preface and Pronunciation Guide

Sing 'n Learn Japanese 1 introduces Japanese language through a collection of favorite children's songs which are designed to teach Japanese language the fun and natural way. It is a well known fact that songs and games enhance language learning. We have carefully chosen 23 traditional and contemporary children's songs that can be used at home and classrooms to teach about Japan and the Japanese language. Both children and adults can enjoy these singable and danceable songs. We have chosen to include the romanization of Japanese, Hiragana and Katakana written system so that the book and music can be used by both beginners as well as intermediate level learners. Words of some songs have been changed or modified to enhance learning.

The pronunciation of Japanese words is based on five vowel sounds: a, i, u, e, and o -- located at the top of each column at the right. These short vowels are pronounced crisply and distinctly making them easy to understand. ("a" as in **ah**, "i" as in **me**, "u" as in **moon**, "e" as in **net**, "o" as in **boat**). Long vowel sounds are written as aa, ii, uu, ee, and oo making them more continuous sounds. For the most part, Japanese consonants sound similar to those in English. "N" is the only consonant that does not have to combine with any vowel and can therefore stand alone (otoosa**n** for father). A double consonant (kk, tt, pp) is reflected by a small "tsu" in hiragana and requires a slight pause between the two consonants as in ga**kk**oo (school).

Japanese nouns reflect neither number nor gender. Verbs are also unaffected by gender or number, and they usually fall at the end of the sentence or phrase. Most of our translations use the singular form of nouns. The Japanese language has many degrees of politeness depending on the person being addressed. The choice of nouns and verbs depends on whether the conversation is with a friend, parent, teacher or even the emperor. A noun may be given more polite distinction if preceded by an "o" as in okaasan vs. kaasan (mother) or ohana vs. hana (flower). In the same light, the suffix "-san" is a title of respect added to a name excluding one's own. It may be used with a female or male name as well as given name or surname.

The written Japanese language involves three different types of characters -- **kanji**, **hiragana**, and **katakana**. **Kanji** are pictographs that were borrowed from the Chinese language and adapted to fit Japanese. Each character has a specific meaning but may be pronounced in different ways depending on its usage or its combination with other characters. Today there are close to 2000 commonly used kanji. The two phonetic systems collectively called **kana** -- hiragana and katakana -- represent the same 46 basic sounds, plus some other combinations of sounds. **Katakana** is used for all foreign words, foreign names, and sounds as in the noise that a frog makes or of rain on an umbrella. **Hiragana** is used with kanji to write verb endings, particles, conjunctions, and essentially anything not written in kanji or katakana. We have included the Kana charts on the next page.

The romanized version of the Japanese language is great for beginners to learn the difficult language. As in English, Japanese may be written from right to left horizontally, or it is also commonly written vertically from top to bottom and moving from the right side of the page to the left. In Japan, most children learn Hiragana first, followed by Katakana. Kanji is taught later.

Listen to the songs often to improve your listening comprehension and pronunciation. Follow the lyrics and then sing along. You can add motions and variations to the songs for countless hours of fun learning. All background and cultural notes and activity guides are on pages 31 and 32. More advanced songs which are organized by Japanese holidays and festivals are collected in the second volume, Sing 'n Learn Japanese 2.

Japanese Writing System
Hiragana (Katakana)

Basic Syllables and "n"

a あ(ア)	i い(イ)	u う(ウ)	e え(エ)	o お(オ)
ka か(カ)	ki き(キ)	ku く(ク)	ke け(ケ)	ko こ(コ)
sa さ(サ)	shi し(シ)	su す(ス)	se せ(セ)	so そ(ソ)
ta た(タ)	chi ち(チ)	tsu つ(ツ)	te て(テ)	to と(ト)
na な(ナ)	ni に(ニ)	nu ぬ(ヌ)	ne ね(ネ)	no の(ノ)
ha は(ハ)	hi ひ(ヒ)	hu ふ(フ)	he へ(ヘ)	ho ほ(ホ)
ma ま(マ)	mi み(ミ)	mu む(ム)	me め(メ)	mo も(モ)
ya や(ヤ)		yu ゆ(ユ)		yo よ(ヨ)
ra ら(ラ)	ri り(リ)	ru る(ル)	re れ(レ)	ro ろ(ロ)
wa わ(ワ)				o を(ヲ)
n ん(ン)				

Modified Syllables

ga が(ガ)	gi ぎ(ギ)	gu ぐ(グ)	ge げ(ゲ)	go ご(ゴ)
za ざ(ザ)	ji じ(ジ)	zu ず(ズ)	ze ぜ(ゼ)	zo ぞ(ゾ)
da だ(ダ)	ji ぢ(ヂ)	zu づ(ヅ)	de で(デ)	do ど(ド)
ba ば(バ)	bi び(ビ)	bu ぶ(ブ)	be べ(ベ)	bo ぼ(ボ)
pa ぱ(パ)	pi ぴ(ピ)	pu ぷ(プ)	pe ぺ(ペ)	po ぽ(ポ)

Modified Syllables: Consonants with ya, yu, and yo

kya きゃ(キャ)	kyu きゅ(キュ)	kyo きょ(キョ)
sha しゃ(シャ)	shu しゅ(シュ)	sho しょ(ショ)
cha ちゃ(チャ)	chu ちゅ(チュ)	cho ちょ(チョ)
nya にゃ(ニャ)	nyu にゅ(ニュ)	nyo にょ(ニョ)
hya ひゃ(ヒャ)	hyu ひゅ(ヒュ)	hyo ひょ(ヒョ)
mya みゃ(ミャ)	myu みゅ(ミュ)	myo みょ(ミョ)
rya りゃ(リャ)	ryu りゅ(リュ)	ryo りょ(リョ)
gya ぎゃ(ギャ)	gyu ぎゅ(ギュ)	gyo ぎょ(ギョ)
ja じゃ(ジャ)	ju じゅ(ジュ)	jo じょ(ジョ)
bya びゃ(ビャ)	byu びゅ(ビュ)	byo びょ(ビョ)
pya ぴゃ(ピャ)	pyu ぴゅ(ピュ)	pyo ぴょ(ピョ)

4

どこですか
Doko desu ka

エリカちゃん　エリカちゃん　どこにいます
Erica-chan　　Erica-chan　doko ni imasu

ここです　ここです　ここにいます
Koko desu koko desu　koko ni imasu

おはようございます
Ohayoo　gozaimasu

ピーター　ピーター　どこにいます
Peter　　Peter　doko ni imasu

ここです　ここです　ここにいます
Koko desu koko desu　koko ni imasu

こんにちは
Konnichi wa

まりさん　まりさん　どこにいます
Mari-san　Mari-san　doko ni imasu

ここです　ここです　ここにいます
Koko desu koko desu　koko ni imasu

こんばんは
Konban wa

Where Are You?

Little Erika, little Erika, where are you?
Here I am, here I am, I'm here.
Good morning!

Peter, Peter, where are you?
Here I am, here I am, I'm here.
Good day! (Hello!)

Ms. Mari, Ms. Mari, where are you?
Here I am, here I am, I'm here.
Good evening!

こぶたぬきつねこ
Ko bu ta nu ki tsu ne ko

こぶた	こぶた	たぬき	たぬき
Kobuta	**kobuta**	**tanuki**	**tanuki**

きつね	きつね	ねこ	ねこ
Kitsune	**kitsune**	**neko**	**neko**

Piglet, Raccoon, Fox, Cat

Piglet, piglet, raccoon, raccoon,
Fox, fox, cat, cat.

くまさん
Kuma-san

くまさん	くまさん	まわれみぎ
Kuma-san	kuma-san	maware migi
くまさん	くまさん	りょうてを ついて
Kuma-san	kuma-san	ryoote o　tsuite
くまさん	くまさん	かたあし あげて
Kuma-san	kuma-san	kataashi　agete
くまさん	くまさん	さようなら
Kuma-san	kuma-san	sayoonara

Bear

Bear, Bear, turn to the right.
Bear, Bear, put both hands on the ground.
Bear, Bear, raise your leg.
Bear, Bear, goodbye.

ブン ブン ブン
Bun　Bun　Bun

ブン ブン ブン はちが とぶ
Bun　bun　bun　hachi ga tobu

おいけの まわりに のばらが さいたよ
Oike no　　mawarini nobara ga　saita yo

ブン ブン ブン はちが とぶ
Bun　bun　bun　hachi ga tobu

A Flying Bee

Buzz, buzz, buzz, a bee is flying.
Around the pond, pretty roses are blooming.
Buzz, buzz, buzz, a bee is flying.

8

かえるのうた
Kaeru no Uta

かえるの うたが きこえて くるよ
Kaeru no uta ga kikoete kuru yo

クワ クワ クワ クワ
Kwa kwa kwa kwa

ケ ケ ケ ケ ケ ケ ケ ケ
Ke ke ke ke ke ke ke ke

クワ クワ クワ
Kwa kwa kwa

Frog's Song

We can hear the frogs singing,
kwa, kwa, kwa, kwa,
ke, ke, ke, ke,
ke, ke, ke, ke,
kwa, kwa, kwa.

てを たたきましょう
Te o Tatakimashoo

てを たたきましょう
Te o tatakimashoo

タン タン タン タン タン タン
Tan tan tan tan tan tan

あしぶみしましょう
Ashibumi shimashoo

タン タン タン タン タン タン タン
Tan tan tan tan tan tan tan

(Repeat at the beginning of each verse below.)

1. わらいましょう　アッハッハッ
 Waraimashoo a ha ha

 わらいましょう　アッハッハッ
 Waraimashoo a ha ha

 あっはっはっ　アッハッハッ
 A ha ha a ha ha

 ああ　おもしろい
 Aa omoshiroi

2. おこりましょう　プン プン プン
 Okorimashoo pun pun pun

 おこりましょう　プン プン プン
 Okorimashoo pun pun pun

 プン プン プン　プン プン プン
 Pun pun pun pun pun pun

 ああ　おもしろい
 Aa omoshiroi

3. なきましょう　エン エン エン
 Nakimashoo en en en

 なきましょう　エン エン エン
 Nakimashoo en en en

 エン エン エン　エン エン エン
 En en en en en en

 ああ　おもしろい
 Aa omoshiroi

Let's Clap Our Hands

Let's clap our hands.
Clap, clap, clap, clap, clap, clap.
Let's stomp our feet.
Stomp, stomp, stomp, stomp stomp, stomp.
(Repeat at the beginning of each verse below.)

1) Let's laugh out loud. Ha, Ha, Ha.
   Let's laugh out loud. Ha, Ha, Ha.
   Ha, Ha, Ha, Ha, Ha, Ha.
   Oh, how fun it is!

2) Let's get angry. Grr. Grr. Grr.
   Let's get angry. Grr. Grr. Grr.
   Grr. Grr. Grr. Grr. Grr. Grr.
   Oh, how fun it is!

3) Let's cry. Boo hoo. Boo hoo. Boo hoo.
   Let's cry. Boo hoo. Boo hoo. Boo hoo.
   Boo hoo hoo hoo. Boo hoo hoo.
   Oh, how fun it is!

あかい　とり　ことり
Akai　Tori　Kotori

あかい　とり　ことり
Akai　tori　kotori

なぜ　なぜ　あかい
Naze naze　akai

あかい　み　を　たべた
Akai　mi　o　tabeta

あおい　とり　ことり
Aoi　tori　kotori

なぜ　なぜ　あおい
Naze naze　aoi

あおい　み　を　たべた
Aoi　mi　o　tabeta

しろい　とり　ことり
Shiroi　tori　kotori

なぜ　なぜ　しろい
Naze naze　shiroi

しろい　み　を　たべた
Shiroi　mi　o　tabeta

Red Bird, Little Bird

Red bird, little bird,
Why are you so red?
'Cause I ate some red berries.

Blue bird, little bird,
Why are you so blue?
'Cause I ate some blue berries.

White bird, little bird,
Why are you so white?
'Cause I ate some white berries.

ぞうさん
Zoo-san

ぞうさん ぞうさん おはな が ながいのね
Zoo-san　　zoo-san　　ohana　ga　nagai no ne

そうよ かあさんも ながいのよ
Sooyo　　kaasan mo　nagai no yo

ぞうさん ぞうさん だれが すきなの
Zoo-san　　zoo-san　　dare ga　sukina no

あのね かあさんが すきなのよ
Ano ne　　kaasan ga　　sukina no yo

Elephant

Elephant, elephant, your nose is so long.
Yes, my mother's nose is long too.

Elephant, elephant, whom do you like?
Well, I like my mother.

チューリップ
Tulip

さいた　さいた　チューリップの　はなが
Saita　saita　tulip　no hana ga

ならんだ　ならんだ　あか　しろ　きいろ
Naranda　naranda　aka　shiro　kiiro

どの　はな　みても　きれいだな
Dono hana mitemo　kireida na

Tulips

Blooming, blooming, the tulips are in bloom.
All in a row, all in a row, red, white, yellow.
Every flower I see looks so pretty.

つき
Tsuki

でた でた つきが
Deta deta tsuki ga

まるい まるい まんまるい
Marui   marui   manmarui

ぼんの ような つきが
Bon no   yoona   tsuki ga

かくれた くもに
Kakureta   kumo ni

くろい くろい まっくろい
Kuroi   kuroi   makkuroi

すみの ような くもに
Sumino   yoona   kumo ni

The Moon

The moon came out.
A perfectly round moon.
It's as round as a tray.

It's hidden behind a cloud.
A perfectly black cloud.
In a cloud of black ink.

One Chopstick, Two Chopsticks

One chopstick, one chopstick became a mountain.
Two chopsticks, two chopsticks became a pair of eyeglasses.
Three chopsticks, three chopsticks became a jellyfish.
Four chopsticks, four chopsticks became a moustache.
Five chopsticks, five chopsticks became a bird.

 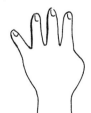  

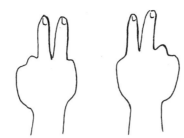

いっぽんばし　にほんばし
Ippon Bashi　Nihon Bashi

いっぽんばし　いっぽんばし　おやまに　なちゃった
Ippon bashi　ippon bashi　oyama ni　nacchatta

にほんばし　にほんばし　めがねに　なっちゃった
Nihon bashi　nihon bashi　megane ni　nacchatta

さんぼんばし　さんぼんばし　くらげに　なっちゃった
Sanbon bashi　sanbon bashi　kurage ni　nacchatta

よんほんばし　よんほんばし　おひげに　なっちゃった
Yonhon bashi　yonhon bashi　ohige ni　nacchatta

ごほんばし　ごほんばし　ことりに　なっちゃった
Gohon bashi　gohon bashi　kotori ni　nacchatta

おうま
Ouma

おうまの おやこは なかよし こよし
Ouma no oyako wa nakayoshi koyoshi

いつでも いっしょに
Itsudemo issho ni

ぽっくり ぽっくり あるく
Pokkuri pokkuri aruku

おうまの かあさん やさしい かあさん
Ouma no kaasan yasashii kaasan

こうまを みながら
Kouma o minagara

ぽっくり ぽっくり あるく
Pokkuri pokkuri aruku

Horses

Mother horse and baby horse are so very close.
Always walking together,
Clip-pity clop, clip-pity clop.

Mother horse is a caring horse.
Watching her baby,
Clip-pity clop, clip-pity clop.

おおきな　たいこ　ちいさな　たいこ
Ookina　　Taiko　Chiisana　Taiko

おおきな　たいこ　ドン　ドン
Ookina　　taiko　　don　　don

ちいさな　たいこ　トン　トン　トン
Chiisana　taiko　　ton　　ton　　ton

おおきな　たいこ　ちいさな　たいこ
Ookina　　taiko　　chiisana　taiko

ドン　ドン　トン　トン　トン
Don　　don　　ton　　ton　　ton

Big Drum, Little Drum

A big drum goes gong, gong.
A little drum goes tap, tap, tap.
Big drum, little drum,
Gong, gong. Tap, tap, tap.

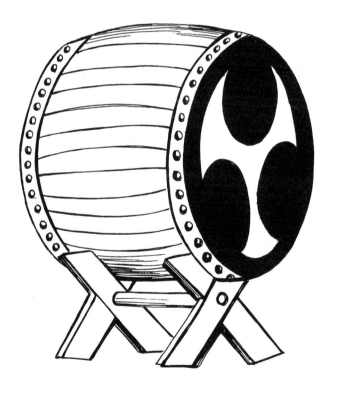

あめふり
Amefuri

あめ あめ ふれ ふれ かあさんが
Ame ame fure fure kaasan ga

じゃのめで おむかえ うれしいな
Janome de omukae ureshiina

ピッチ ピッチ チャップ チャップ
Pitch pitch chap chap

ラン ラン ラン
Ran ran ran

A Rainy Day

Rain, rain. How nice Mother
Brings an umbrella for me!
Pitter-patter, pitter-patter,
Pitter-patter.

だるまさん
Daruma-san

だるまさん だるまさん
Daruma-san daruma-san

にらめっこ しましょ
Niramekko shimasho

わらうと だめよ あっぷっぷっ
Warauto dameyo a-ppu-ppu

Daruma-san

Daruma-san, daruma-san,
Let's have a staring contest.
Don't laugh. A-ppu-ppu.

ゆき
Yuki

ゆきや こんこん あられや こんこん
Yukiya　konkon　arareya　konkon

ふっては ふっては ずんずん つもる
Futtewa　futtewa　zunzun　tsumoru

やまも　のはらも　わたぼうし　かぶり
Yama mo nohara mo watabooshi　kaburi

かれき のこらず はなが さく
Kareki nokorazu hana ga saku

ゆきや こんこん あられや こんこん
Yukiya　konkon　arareya　konkon

ふっても ふっても まだ ふりやまぬ
Futtemo　futtemo　mada furiyamanu

いぬは よろこび にわ かけまわる
Inu wa yorokobi niwa kakemawaru

ねこは　こたつで　まるくなる
Neko wa kotatsu de marukunaru

Snow

Snow is falling, hail is falling,
Falling, falling and piling up.
Mountains and fields both wear white caps.
White flowers bloom even on dead branches.

Snow is falling, hail is falling.
Falling, falling, they never stop.
A dog is happily running in the yard.
A cat crouches by the heater.

うみ
Umi

うみは　ひろいな　おおきいな
Umi wa　hiroina　ookiina
つきが　のぼるし　ひが　しずむ
Tsuki ga noborushi hi ga shizumu

うみは　おおなみ　あおい　なみ
Umi wa　oonami　aoi　nami
ゆれて　どこまで　つづくやら
Yurete　doko made tsuzukuyara

うみに　おふねを　うかばせて
Umi ni　ofune o　ukabasete
いってみたいな　よその　くに
Ittemitaina　yosono　kuni

The Ocean

The ocean is so wide and big.
As the moon comes up, the sun is setting.

The ocean has such big, blue waves.
They roll on and on!

While floating on a boat,
I wish that I could travel to faraway lands.

おおきな くりの きのしたで
Ookina　Kurino Ki no Shita de

おおきな くりの きのしたで
Ookina　kuri no ki no shita de

あなたと わたし たのしく あそびましょう
Anata to　watashi　tanoshiku　asobimashoo

おおきな くりの きのしたで
Ookina　kuri no ki no shita de

Under the Big
Chestnut Tree

Under the big chestnut tree,
Let's play happily together
Under the big chestnut tree.

かたつむり
Katatsumuri

でんでん むし むし かたつむり
Den den mushi mushi katatsumuri

おまえの あたまは どこに ある
Omae no atama wa doko ni aru

つの だせ やり だせ あたま だせ
Tsuno dase   yari dase   atama dase

でんでん むし むし かたつむり
Den den mushi mushi katatsumuri

おまえの めだま は どこに ある
Omae no medama wa doko ni aru

つの だせ やり だせ めだま だせ
Tsuno dase   yari dase   medama dase

Snail

Snail, snail, dear snail,
Where is your head?
Show me your feelers, your horns
and your head.

Snail, snail, dear snail,
Where are your eyes?
Show me your feelers, your horns
and your eyes.

あたまと かたと ひざ
Atama to Kata to Hiza

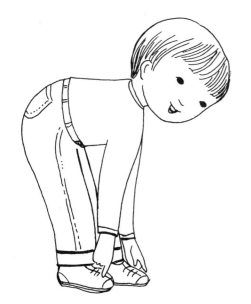

あたま かた ひざ あし ひざ あし
Atama kata hiza ashi hiza ashi

あたま かた ひざ あし ひざ あし
Atama kata hiza ashi hiza ashi

め と みみと くちと はな
Me to mimi to kuchi to hana

あたま かた ひざ あし ひざ あし
Atama kata hiza ashi hiza ashi

Head and Shoulders

Head, shoulders, knees, feet, knees, feet
Head, shoulders, knees, feet, knees, feet
Eyes and ears and mouth and nose.
Head, shoulders, knees, feet, knees, feet.

むすんで ひらいて
Musunde　Hiraite

むすんで ひらいて
Musunde　hiraite

てを うって むすんで
Te o　utte　musunde

また ひらいて てを うって
Mata　hiraite　te o　utte

そのてを うえに
Sono te o　ue ni

むすんで ひらいて
Musunde　hiraite

てを うって むすんで
Te o　utte　musunde

Close Your Hands

Close your hands and open your hands
Clap and close your hands.
Open your hands again and clap your hands
Put your hands up.
Close your hands and open your hands
Clap and close your hands.

きらきら ほしよ
Kirakira Hoshiyo

きらきら ひかる きれいな ほしよ
Kirakira hikaru kireina hoshiyo

おそらの なかで ダイヤモンドの ように
Osorano naka de diamond no yooni

きらきら ひかる きれいな ほしよ
Kirakira hikaru kireina hoshiyo

Twinkle, Twinkle, Star

Twinkle, twinkle, beautiful star,
High up in the sky, sparkling like a diamond.
Twinkle, twinkle, beautiful star.

28

さようなら
Sayoonara

さようなら　さようなら
Sayoonara　　sayoonara
これで　おしまい
Korede　oshimai

また　あした　あいましょう
Mata　ashita　　aimashoo
さようなら　さようなら
Sayoonara　　sayoonara

Good-bye

Good-bye, good-bye.
It's time to go.
Until tomorrow.
Good-bye, good-bye.

bear	kuma
beautiful	kirei
bee	hachi
berry	mi
big	ookii
bird	tori, kotori
black	kuroi
blue	aoi
boat	fune
cat	neko
chopsticks	hashi
cloud	kumo
cute	kawaii
dog	inu
drum	taiko
ear	mimi
elephant	zoo
eye	me
eyeglasses	megane
field	nohara
flower	hana
fly (to)	tobu
foot	ashi
fox	kitsune
frog	kaeru
hand	te
head	atama
horse	ouma
jellyfish	kurage
knee	hiza
leaf	ha, happa
leg	ashi
moon	tsuki
mother	okaasan
mountain	yama
moustache	ohige
mouth	kuchi
nose	hana
ocean	umi
piglet	kobuta
pond	oike
raccoon	tanuki
rain	ame
right	migi
red	akai
shoulder	kata
sky	sora
small	chiisai
snail	katatsumuri
snow	yuki
star	hoshi
sun	hi
tomorrow	ashita
white	shiroi
wide	hiroi
yellow	kiiroi

Numbers

zero	rei, zero
one	ichi
two	ni
three	san
four	shi, yon
five	go
six	roku
seven	shichi, nana
eight	hachi
nine	kyuu, ku
ten	juu
eleven	juu-ichi
twenty	ni-juu
one hundred	hyaku
one thousand	sen

Animals

piglet	kobuta
pig	buta
fox	kitsune
raccoon	tanuki
cat	neko
horse	ouma
bird	tori, kotori
bee	hachi
bear	kuma
snail	katatsumuri
dog	inu
elephant	zoo
jellyfish	kurage
frog	kaeru
rabbit	usagi

Colors

red	akai	brown	chairo
blue	aoi	pink	pinku
yellow	kiiroi	white	shiroi
green	midori	orange	orenji
black	kuroi		
purple	murasaki		

Family

mother	okaasan
father	otoosan
older brother	oniisan
older sister	oneesan
baby	akachan
grandmother	obaasan
grandfather	ojiisan
aunt	obasan
uncle	ojisan
teacher	sensei
friend	tomodachi

Greetings

Good morning.	Ohayoo gozaimasu.
Hello.	Kon-nichiwa.
Good evening.	Konbanwa.
Goodbye.	Sayoonara.
Good night.	Oyasumi nasai.
Thank you (very much).	Arigatoo (gozaimasu).
You're welcome.	Doo itashimasite.
My name is ...	Namae wa ... desu.
I'm home.	Tadaima.
Welcome home.	Okaeri nasai.
Congratulations.	Omedetoo gozaimasu.
How are you?	Ogenki desu ka.
Fine, thanks.	Genki desu.
Excuse me. I'm sorry.	Sumimasen.
I will receive the meal. (before eating)	Itadakimasu.
Thanks for the meal. (after eating)	Gochisoosama (deshita).

Body Parts

head	atama
shoulder	kata
arm	ude
hand	te
finger	yubi
face	kao
eye	me
ear	mimi
nose	hana
mouth	kuchi
tooth	ha
tongue	shita
leg/foot	ashi
knee	hiza

Seasons

spring	haru
summer	natsu
fall	aki
winter	fuyu

Directions

Where?	doko
right	migi
left	hidari
up, over	ue
down, under	shita
behind	ushiro
front	mae
inside	naka
outside	soto

Sing 'n Learn Japanese 1 introduces Japanese in the context of many popular and fun tunes sung in Japan. The songs are specially chosen to cover important concepts such as greetings, family, numbers, colors, action verbs, body parts, and animals. Each lyric is written in Kana, romanized Japanese, anpd English. Illustrations enhance the understanding of the song and the Japanese culture. With this activity guide, you can use the songs and books not only for language learning but also for culture. Sing 'n Learn Japanese 2 contains over 20 songs on festivals, culture and more vocabulary.

1. Where Are You?   *Page 4*

Teaches greetings, name and places. Have the children stand in a circle holding hands with an adult standing in the middle. The child whose name is called moves one step inside to respond "I'm here.". Repeat calling on other children. We chose to use both "chan" after a name to call small children and "san" as a polite form to show variation of the name calling. "imasu" is used to say "there is" for living things while "arimasu" is used to say "there is" for objects.

2. Piglet, Raccoon, Fox, Cat   *Page 6*

This is a Japanese "shiritori" which uses the last letter of one word to form the first letter of the next word in a melody. This is similar to English rhyming. Start with the first word "kobuta" and have the children repeat. Then, say the next word using the last letter of the previous word "tanuki"and so on. Have the kids make their own combinations up. Great for vocabulary building and fun to play.

3. Bear   *Page 7*

Great to practice parts of the body and directions (right, left, up, down). In a circle, the teacher sings and the children follow the instructions. Change the movement to say "turn to the left" or "put both hands on your head." If the children make a mistake, have them sit inside the circle until the last one is left standing.

4. A Flying Bee   *Page 8*

An introduction to animal sounds. Very easy melody and easy words to pronounce. Have the children talk about the signs of spring.

5. Frog's Song   *Page 9*

Frogs are a sign of summer's arrival. People hear the frogs and know the rainy season is near. They believe that frogs are calling for the rain needed to plant the rice seedlings. You can make frog origami by folding papers.

6. Let's Clap Our Hands   *Page 10*

A joyful, active song where children can clap their hands and stomp their feet to learn the parts of the body. The song also teaches the words which express one's feelings such as angry, sad or happy.

7. Red Bird, Little Bird   *Page 12*

This is a very popular song which introduces colors and adjectives. Substitute other colors and have the children respond to the question "why are you so...?". Use pictures or cut-outs of birds to reinforce the lyrics.

8. Elephant   *Page 13*

One of the many songs to show the warm, tender relationship between mother and child. In Japan a mother's role is very important as children are growing up. They spend a lot of time with them for security.

9. Tulips   *Page 14*

A song to celebrate spring. Substitute other flowers and colors. Use cut-outs or have the children make their own flowers. The Japanese pronunciation of the tulip's katakana writing is "Chuuripu." We have chosen to use Tulip as it is very difficult to learn borrowed English words used in Japan for a beginner.

10. The Moon   *Page 15*

A celebration of the Moon Festival. In September when the sky is most clear, Japanese families watch the full moon from the backyard or by the window. It is thought to purify the evils of the world. Offerings of rice dumplings (tsukimi dango) and arrangements of grass from fields would be left for the moon.

11. One Chopstick, Two Chopsticks   *Page 16*

Use your fingers to make the "chopstick" shapes given in the song. Touch one finger from each hand together to form a mountain, two fingers from each hand to form eyeglasses, etc. Or, use chopsticks or popsicle sticks to create figures. Have the children come up with other creative shapes. Practice counting numbers.

12. Horses *Page 18*

Another popular children's song in Japan featuring mother and child. Ask children what they like to do with their mothers or even what activities other animals do with their mothers -- dogs running together, cats walking, cows sitting under a tree, etc.

13. Big Drum, Little Drum *Page 19*

In Japan people have many festivals (matsuri) for the shrines and temples that were originally constructed to protect the villages and its inhabitants. Taiko (drums) are the oldest and most important instruments in Japan especially for the local festivals. The beat of the drums inspires and excites people. Have the children stand in a wide circle repeating the part of the large drum then move the circle in close to clap the beat of the small drum. Move in and out as the beats are repeated. Or have the girls be one drum while the boys are the other.

14. A Rainy Day *Page 20*

Rainy days in Japan are frequent in June. In the song, a mother picks her child up from school with an umbrella. The umbrellas used to be made of bamboo and waxed paper or cloth and were much larger to cover both mother and child.

15. Daruma-san *Page 21*

Daruma dolls are one of the folk toys representing a Buddhist priest Bodhidharma, who is said to have meditated in a cave wrapped in a red blanket under severe conditions. The egg-shaped dolls are usually made of papier-mache on a bamboo frame and weighted in the center. Daruma-san is a symbol of endurance because of its ability to upright itself after being pushed over. People who want to achieve a goal will paint one eye before placing the doll on the family shrine. When they meet their goal or wish, the other eye is then painted. The eyes are painted in any expression -- sad, rounded, scary-looking, smiling, etc. Children like to play "Niramekko", a staring contest played by making faces -- the first to laugh loses. Let the children have their own staring contest or have them paint/draw their own daruma dolls' eyes.

16. Snow *Page 22*

A winter song expressing children's love of snow and playing in snow. Discuss what children like to do in the snow or if they've ever seen it or have them collect pictures of winter scenes. "Kotatsu" is a heater beneath a table covered with a padded quilt (futon). Many people can sit around the table with their legs covered by the warm futon as an economical way of keeping warm in the winter. Kotatsu is a popular method of heating today.

17. The Ocean *Page 23*

Observing the ocean, children are inspired to dream of faraway lands and cultures. Ask what countries/cultures children would like to travel to or visit, how they might get there (boat, plane, train, car), and what they would like to see.

18. Under the Big Chestnut Tree *Page 24*

An activity-based song that Japanese use to get children acquainted with each other. Have the children stand in a big circle facing the middle. While making the shape of a tree with both hands above their heads, they sing "under the big chestnut tree". Then, have them pair off and face each other while singing "you and I will play joyfully". Then, repeat first line while back in original position.

19. Snail *Page 25*

Another observation in spring when many snails appear. They pull their feelers and bodies into the shell when touched, making children beg to show their heads again.

20. Head & Shoulders *Page 26*

A lively song for children to practice the parts of the body. While singing, they can point to the parts of the body mentioned. Start out slow and then speed up as the children become more familiar with the vocabulary.

21. Close Your Hands *Page 27*

This is a popular song virtually every child learns in Japan. Many of the children's songs taught in Japan have famous melodies which originated from Europe. A simple, playful song that can be used to learn the parts of the body. Substitute other movements such as put your hands down or put your hands on your head or on your mouth.

22. Twinkle, Twinkle *Page 28*

There are many different versions of "Twinkle Twinkle Little" Star in Japan. We chose this song for its simplicity and repetition. Have the kids wave their hands while singing to simulate the twinkling stars.

23. Good-bye *Page 29*

A song to teach phrases associated with saying good-bye. Instead of "tomorrow (ashita)", substitute "next week (raishuu)", "next month (raigetsu)", the days of the week, the seasons or any other time period.